This book of Beach Doodles belongs to:

_____

Doodle your own self-portrait.

Book design: Charla Pettingill

Scanner Magician Extraordinaire: Elizabeth Kidder

First Edition

ISBN: 978-1-938093-04-3

Printed in China

CPSIA Compliance Information: Batch #091512DP
For further information contact Duo Press, LLC at info@duopressbooks.com

For A & P

duopress
www.duopressbooks.com

Beach DOODLES

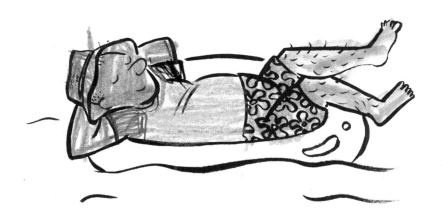

By Puck • Illustrations by Violet Lemay and Paige Garrison

duopress

Ready?

Go!

It's hot at the beach. **Doodle an umbrella.**

It's a nice day! Doodle a family enjoying the beach.

Oh no, a rain shower!
Everybody under the umbrella!

The sun is back, but it is windy!

Now it's getting late. Doodle some stars!

These **crabs** need claws.

What's in the **beach bag?**

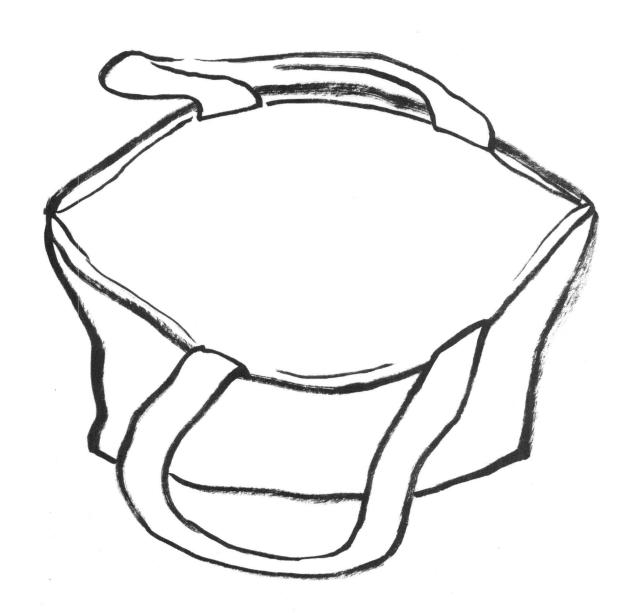

Who is **underwater?**

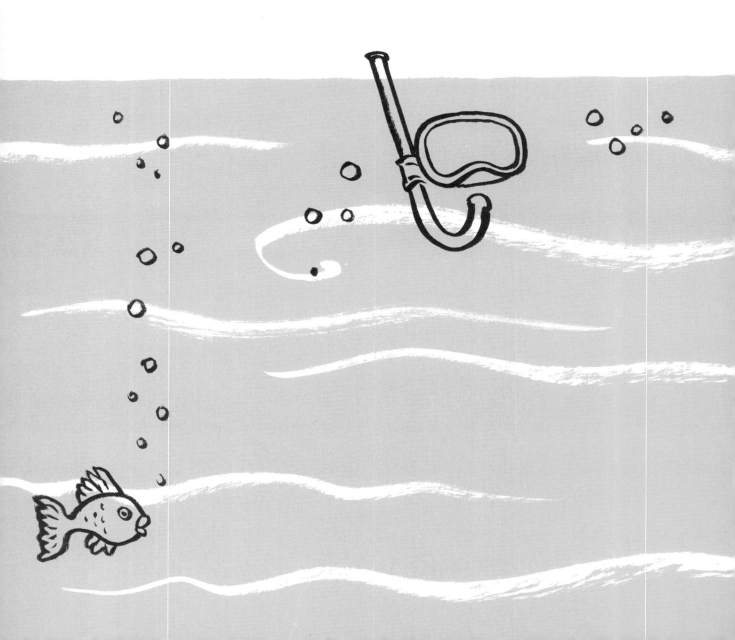

Take the Doodle Challenge:
Draw a starfish using one single line.

Look for four more Doodle Challenges ahead!

Doodle something on this island.

People on this boat need faces.

Doodle some **surfers** riding the waves!

Doodle yourself doing something crazy on the beach.

Doodle a family leaving the beach.

Draw lots of flowers on this **Hawaiian shirt!**

Now draw lots of **sea animals** on this shirt!

Who ate this?

Take the **Doodle Challenge:**
Draw a starfish with your eyes closed.

Look for three more Doodle Challenges ahead!

This food truck has yummy treats.
Doodle your favorite!

This lady has been in the sun a long time. **Doodle** her tan.

Who is buried in the sand?

Doodle a **sand castle!**

It's **movie night** at the beach.
What's showing tonight? Who's watching?

Who is riding the ATV?

Scan this for more beach vehicles to doodle.

Doodle a lot of people on the **boardwalk.**

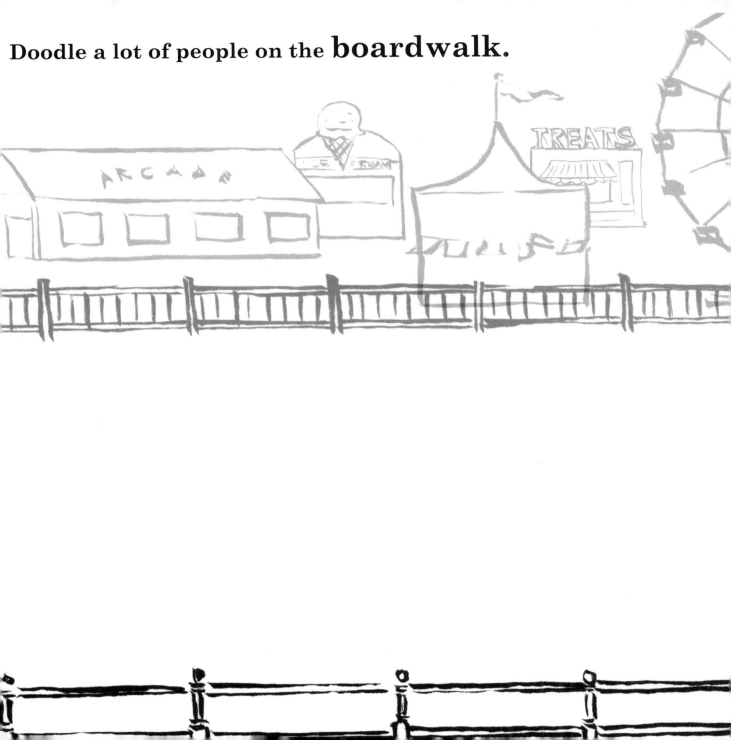

Decorate your baseball hat.

Doodle a lot of people on the **boardwalk.**

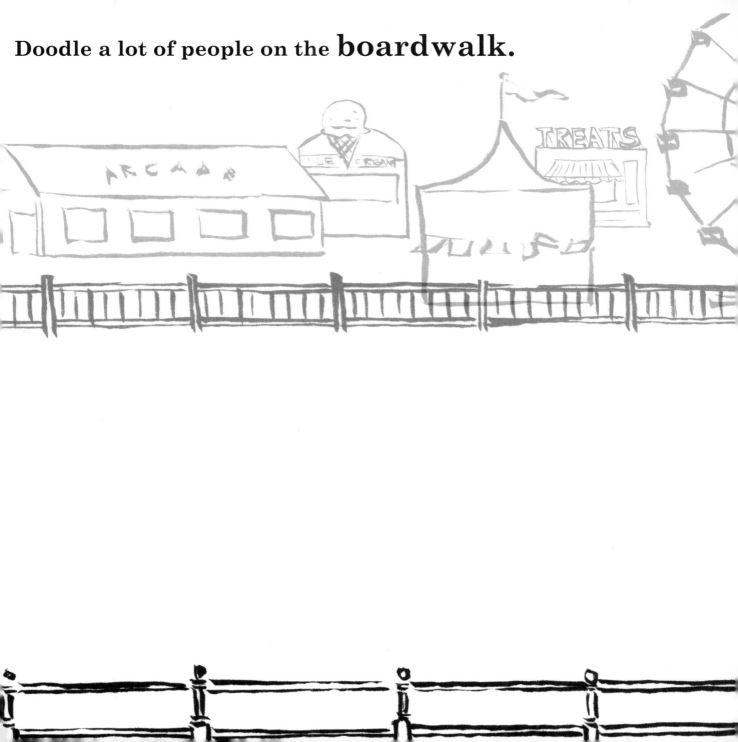

Decorate your baseball hat.

What did they **catch?**

Who is eating at the **picnic table?**

What's on the **banner?**

Who is playing ball at the beach?

These **birds** need bodies.

Doodle **funny sunglasses** on these kids.

What can you see in your **binoculars?**

Finish the whale!

This boy needs a **swimsuit**.

This **girl,** too!

This **scuba diver** needs your help.

BLUE

This **monkey** wants to be a scuba diver!

Take the **Doodle Challenge:**

Draw a starfish with your left hand (especially if you are right-handed!).

Look for two more Doodle Challenges ahead!

Doodle some birds on the pilings.

These kids are **flying kites!**

Draw the cover of your own book.

Doodle yourself **on top** of this waterskiing pyramid!

Why is the **scuba diver** so surprised?

Doodle some volleyball players!

Where is the net? Doodle it!

This lifeguard needs a chair!

Scan this for more lifeguards in action to doodle.

Everybody is waiting in line.

Take the Doodle Challenge:

Draw a starfish with your right hand (especially if you are left-handed!).

Look for one more Doodle Challenge ahead!

What's for sale at the **souvenir stores?**

Doodle a beach sign.

Who (or what) caught the **Frisbee?**

Draw a **treasure** map.

Complete this **strong man!**

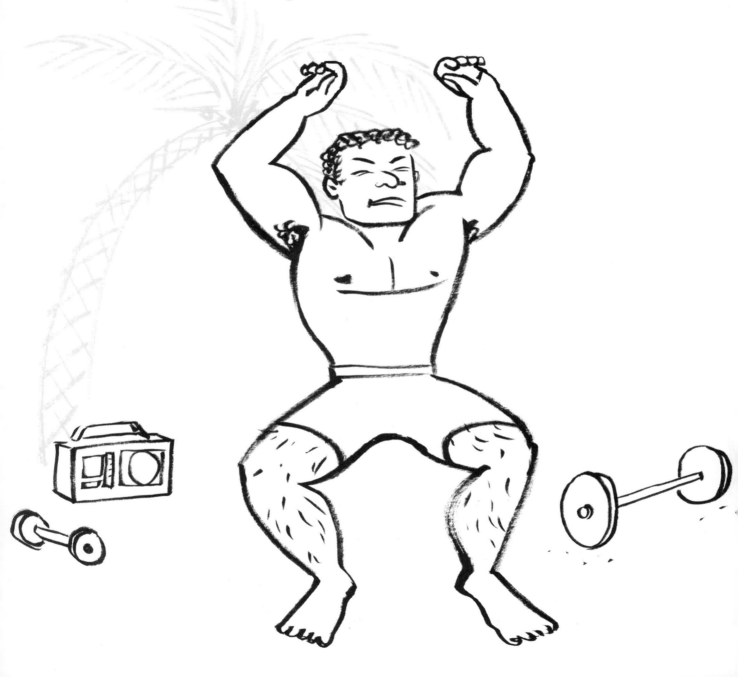

Now this **strong woman!**

Doodle a gorilla (or any other animal) waterskiing.

Doodle a ship inside the bottle.

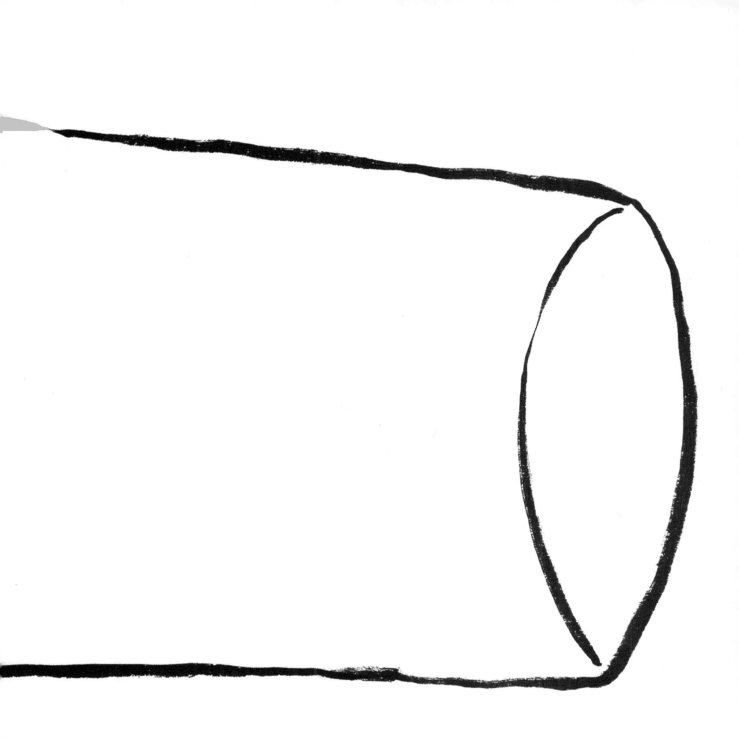

Doodle some **sunbathers.**

How many **beach balls** can you fit in this page?

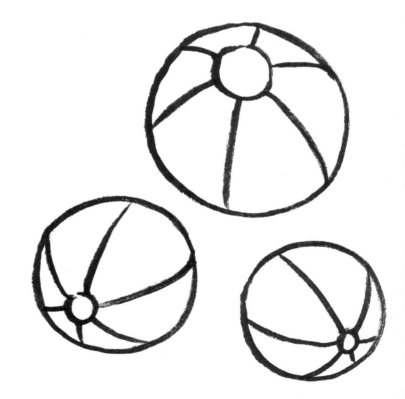

Do you see a ship? Is it a pirate ship?

This bonfire needs fire!

It's a **beach soccer** match!

Who is riding in the **submarine?**

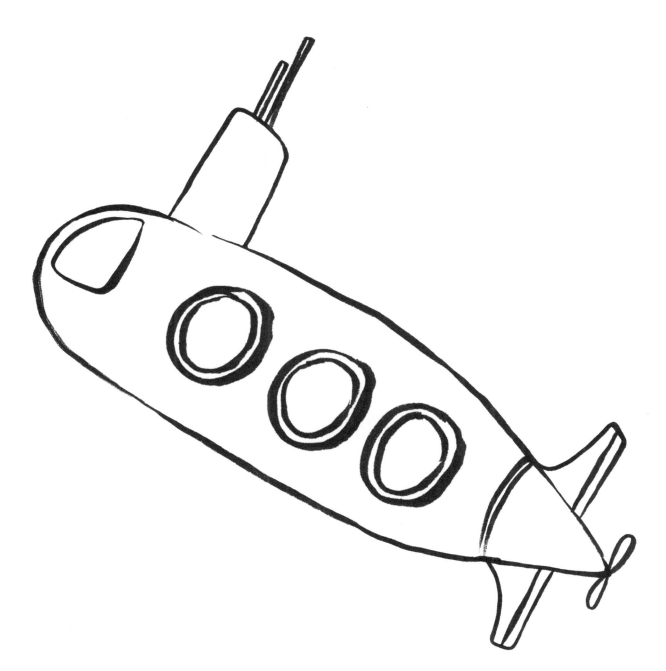

This boy needs a shadow. Doodle it!

What's making these shadows?

What's happening at the **dock?**

What's on the grill?

Take the Doodle Challenge:

Draw two starfish at the same time.

You will need both hands and two pencils!

Doodle the sails on this boat!

Decorate these boogie boards.

Who is riding the waves?

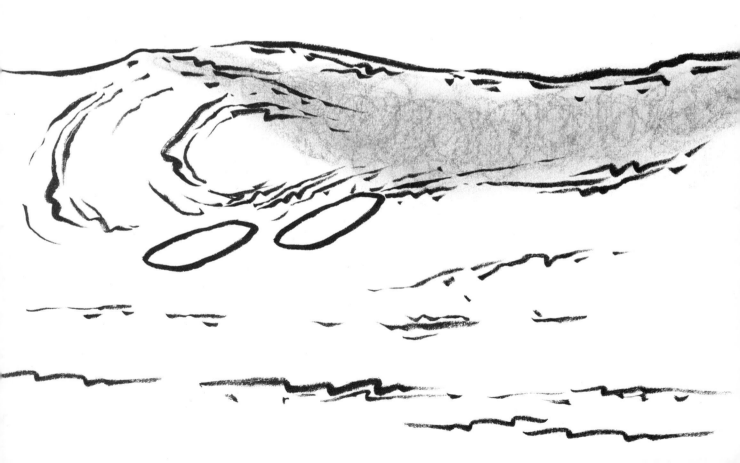

Who is riding the tube?

Fill this jar with **seashells.**

This shark **needs teeth!**

Doodle a **colorful umbrella** for this drink.

Fill this **huge** hamburger!

These **seashells** need color.

Scan this for more seashells to doodle.

Doodle some **beach towels** over this clothesline.

Doodle some sea creatures.

Doodle some hot air balloons over the ocean!

It's a water gun battle!

Who is eating the **watermelon?**

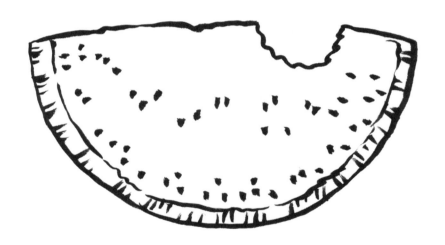

Scan this for more yummy beach foods to doodle.

This person **needs a dog.**

Make this guy the **hairiest** man on the beach.

Draw a kid **taking a nap.**

It's the 4th of July.
Doodle tons of fireworks!

These **horses** need riders.

Draw some hotels along the beach.

The Shell

Fill this **album** with your beach memories.

These kids are **jumping waves!**

Whose **footprints** are these?

Doodle some **constellations** in the sky!